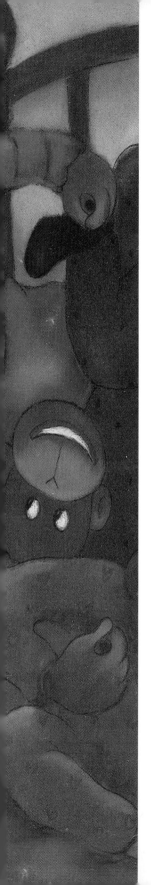

Too Silly!

Ron Benson
Lynn Bryan
Kim Newlove
Liz Stenson
Iris Zammit

CONSULTANTS
Florence Brown
Estella Clayton
Susan Elliott-Johns
Charolette Player
Shari Schwartz
Lynn Swanson
Helen Tomassini
Debbie Toope

AVONDALE SCHOOL

Prentice Hall Ginn

Contents

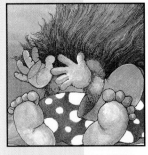

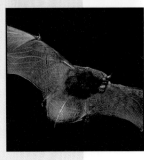

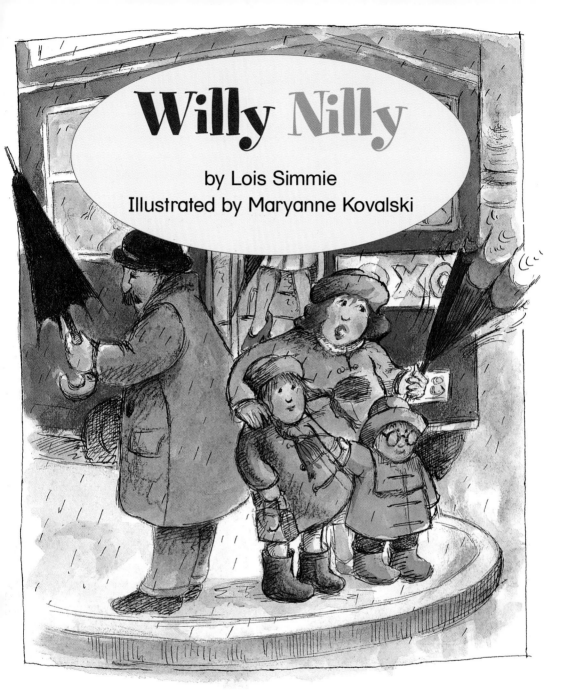

Willy Nilly

by Lois Simmie

Illustrated by Maryanne Kovalski

Milly went to Piccadilly,
Willy went along;

Milly got some piccalilli,
Willy got a song.

4

Milly went back home again,
Willy went along;

Milly ate her piccalilli,
Willy sang his song.

Me

by Nancy Davidson

Illustrated by Carlos Freire

Ten little fingers
And ten little toes.

Two little ears
And a mouth and a nose.

Two little eyes
That shine so bright.

Two little arms
To hug you tight.

Put them together
And what have you got?

11

You've got ME, baby,
And that's a lot!

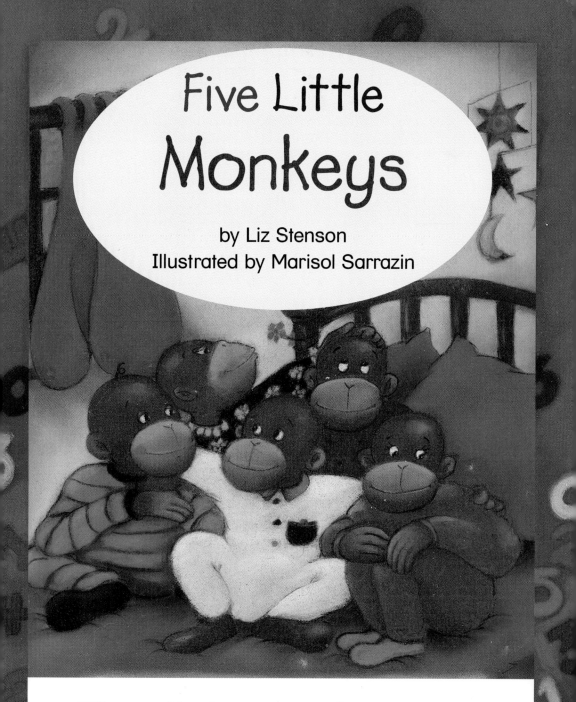

Five Little
Monkeys

by Liz Stenson

Illustrated by Marisol Sarrazin

Five little monkeys
sitting on the bed.

One jumped off.
"Too noisy!" he said.

Four little monkeys
sitting on the bed.

One jumped off.
"Too silly!" she said.

Three little monkeys
sitting on the bed.

One jumped off.
"Too smelly!" he said.

Two little monkeys
sitting on the bed.

Too grumpy!

One jumped off.
"Too grumpy!" she said.

One little monkey
sitting on the bed.

He jumped off.
"I'm lonely!" he said.

Twinkle, Twinkle

by Lewis Carroll

Twinkle, twinkle, little bat!
How I wonder what you're at!

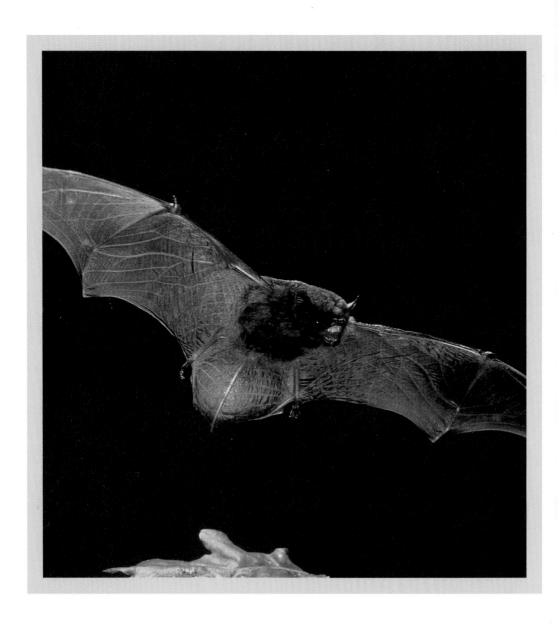

Up above the world you fly,
Like a tea-tray in the sky.